sale .99

D1517245

Cherry-Blossoms

JAPANESE HAIKU
SERIES III

TRANSLATIONS OF
POEMS BY BASHO·
BUSON·ISSA·SHIKI
AND OTHERS

THE PETER
PAUPER PRESS
MOUNT VERNON · NEW YORK

A NOTE ON THIS BOOK OF HAIKU

In Japan cherry-blossoms are a favorite subject of paintings and poems, and are indeed a symbol to the Japanese people of the transitory delight of the "floating world" — as they have called this life on earth. For cherry-blossoms last only three days, and the Buddhist Japanese thinks of his own life as an equally brief flowering in the endless cycle of reincarnation and dissolution.

Because the *haiku* is a poem only seventeen syllables long, and is usually a brief poignant insight into the universality of this endless cycle, the title *Cherry-Blossoms* has been given to this our third collection of *haiku* translations.

Japanese poets of the present continue to write *haiku*: Harold G. Henderson has estimated that perhaps a million new *haiku* are published commercially in magazines each year. But the present collection is taken from the famous poets of the past. Thus the reader will find the names Basho, Buson, Issa and Shiki much in evidence, for these four are the greatest practitioners. A few facts about these men, and a discussion of the difficulties of *haiku* translation, are to be found in our two previous collections.

Here it is necessary only to remind the reader that the poems are not intended to be clear statements. They are fleeting responses or impressions which usually illuminate the poet's awareness — and our own — of the identity of life on different planes. It is the Buddhist doctrine (and most of these poets are Zen Buddhists) that all things and creatures in this world are temporary manifestations risen from the eternal, infinite ocean of Life; and that everything, — from a mountain peak to a cherry-blossom, from a beautiful girl to the little excrement of a bird, — is a part of the universal and inter-related brotherhood of creation.

Of course, not all these poems have this subtle quality. There are a number purely humorous or descriptive.

The *haiku* almost always has a season key-word. Here these have often been omitted, but the poems are arranged by seasons. Since the New Year traditionally begins the Spring, a few cold poems start the book; but the snow soon melts and leaves and blossoms appear.

The interested reader is referred to our *Japanese Haiku*: Series I, *The Four Seasons*, Haiku Series II, and *Haiku Harvest*, Series IV.

Cherry-Blossoms

DECORATIONS AND
LETTERING BY
JEFF HILL

Spring

NEW YEAR'S EVE
I CAN SNORE IN PEACE . . .
　THE NEW YEAR
　　WON'T CONFRONT ME
TILL TOMORROW NOON
　　　　　　BUSON

NEW YEAR'S DAY . . . POET
　THOUGH I BE
　　I'LL PROUDLY WEAR
MY FATHER'S SCABBARD
　　　　　　KYORAI

IN THE NEW YEAR DAWN
　SOLEMN AND
　　DELIBERATE
TALL CRANES GO MARCHING
　　　　　KIKAKU

FROM THE MOUNTAIN PASS
   SEE THE SUNLIT
   CASTLE TOWN . . .
FLYING NEW-YEAR KITES
           TAIGI

SEEING MY BIRTH-CORD
KEPT AT OUR OLD
   NATIVE PLACE . . .
NEW YEAR'S DAY I WEPT
          BASHO

NO YOU DON'T! GET OUT! . . .
   THUS THEY WARMLY
   WELCOMED ME
TO THEIR NEW-YEAR FEAST
          ROTSU

SNOW IS MELTING . . .
   FAR IN THE MISTED
   MOUNTAINS
A CAW-CAWING CROW
          GYODAI

7

SPRING AT EARLY DAWN . . .
   ON THE TIPS OF
   BARLEY LEAVES
LITTLE LAST PALE FROST
            ONITSURA

UP FROM APRIL SNOW
   RISING UDO SPROUTS . . .
   TENDER
PURPLE SUCCULENT
            BASHO

AT DEAR BASHO'S GRAVE
   PALE THIN TRANSIENTS
   WE PAUSE . . .
SPRING MIST, SAD PUPIL
            JOSO

HEAR THOSE BABY MICE
   HUDDLED IN THEIR
   NEST . . . PEEPING
TO THE SPARROWLETS
            BASHO

ABOVE THE HAMLET:
  GREEN THE SILENT
  BAMBOO-GROVE . . .
WHITE LINGERING SNOW
                    TAIGI

SPRING COBALT OCEAN . . .
  ACROSS SNOW-WHITE
  MOUNTAINS FLY
BLACK RETURNING BIRDS
                    SHIKI

IMMEDIATELY . . .
  ON THEIR SPRING
  RETURN TIRELESS
SWALLOWS ZIG-ZAGGING
                    TAIGI

SEE: OUR CANDLELIGHT
  ILLUMINATES
  THE SAPLING'S
FRESH-UNFOLDED GOLD
                    BUSON

TROOPS OF TOURISTS COME
   FOR APRIL
    FLOWER-VIEWING . . .
OH, THEY'RE SPARROW-MEN
            BASHO

GUSTY SPRING BREEZES . . .
   BUT THE STUBBORN
    PLUM BUDS STILL
GRIPPING THEIR THIN TWIGS
          ONITSURA

SPRING UNFOLDS ANEW . . .
   NOW IN MY SECOND
    CHILDHOOD
FOLLY, FOLLY, TOO
            ISSA

BONY BRUSHWOOD TWIGS
   CUT DOWN AND STACKED
    IN BUNCHES . . .
YET BRAVELY BUDDING
          BONCHO

PLACING THE KITTEN
   TO WEIGH HER
    ON THE BALANCE . . .
SHE WENT ON PLAYING

       ISSA

SPRING EVENING BEACH . . .
   HELPING FISHERMEN
    UNLOAD
LIVING SEA-TREASURE

       RANKO

IT IS SPRING AGAIN . . .
   GAY IN THE GARDEN
    GATHER
SUN-BATHING SPARROWS

       ONITSURA

TREMENDOUS FORCES . . .
   STONE-PILED FENCE
    ALL TUMBLED DOWN
BY TWO CATS IN LOVE

       SHIKI

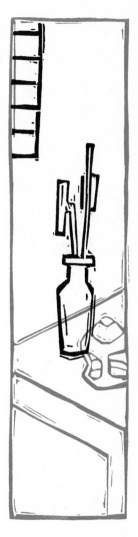

AFTER THE SHOWER . . .
   SPRING-ENCHANTED
   SPARROW-FOLK
CHATTER ON THE EAVES
               UKO

SILENT CHERRY-BLOOM . . .
   AGAIN WITH YOUR
   OLD ELOQUENCE
ADDRESS MY INNER EAR
              ONITSURA

HAVING SCOURED MY SKIN
   AND BOWED MY SKULL
   TO BUDDHA . . .
NOW FOR CHERRY-BLOOM!
              ISSA

AFTERNOON GARDEN . . .
   PLANTING PERHAPS
   SEVEN SEEDS . . .
I'M CONVALESCENT!
              SHIKI

THIS BABY . . . EVEN
WHEN WE SHOW HIM
CHERRY BUDS . . .
OPENS EAGER LIPS

SEIFU-JO

MOUNTAIN-TOP OF CLOUDS
TOWERING BEHIND
THE HEDGE . . .
OR A FLOWERING PLUM?

SHIRO

DANCING: THE FOX TREADS
AMONG THE PALE
NARCISSI
IN GARDEN MOONLIGHT

BUSON

AFTER SPRING SUNSET
MIST RISES FROM
THE RIVER . . .
SPREADING LIKE A FLOOD

CHORA

13

THEN THE PEONIES
   EXTINGUISHING
   ALL OTHERS . . .
OPENED THEIR PETALS
KIICHI

ENDLESS MAYTIME RAIN . . .
   SNEAKING BACK ONE
   NIGHT, THE MOON
PERCHED IN THE PINE-TREE
RANKO

NOW THAT I AM OLD
   EVEN TENDER DAYS
   OF SPRING
SEE . . . CAN MAKE ME CRY
ISSA

BEAUTIFUL LADY
   BUFFETED BY RUDE
   SPRING WINDS . . . WHAT
SWEET STORM YOU MAKE!
KITO

14

ON THE SHINING ROOF
   THE BOY'S ABANDONED
   STRING-BALL
SOAKING UP SPRING RAIN
               BUSON

SWEET SPRING SHOWER . . .
   ENOUGH TO WET
   THE TINY SHELLS
ON THIS LITTLE BEACH
               BUSON

ERE SPRING GUESTS ARRIVE
   WE LIGHT THE
   SUPPER CANDLES
EACH FROM SHINING EACH
               BUSON

DULL-DREARY RAIN-DAY . . .
   DRIPPING PAST
   MY GATE A GIRL
BEARING IRISES
            SHINTOKU

15

YES : THE YOUNG SPARROWS
   IF YOU TREAT THEM
   TENDERLY . . .
THANK YOU WITH DROPPINGS
                 ISSA

FOLLOWING THE BANK . . .
   FOR MILES NO RIVER-
   SPANNING BRIDGE
THIS LONG SPRING DAY
                 SHIKI

AT TAKIGUCHI
   VOICES CALLING
   FOR A LIGHT . . .
DARKENING SPRING RAIN
                BUSON

PATTERING SHOWER . . .
   THEY ARE PUTTING
   OUT THE LAMPS
ALL DOWN DOLL-SHOP LANE
                BUSON

FLOODED PADDY-FIELDS . . .
   THE LAKE HAS COME
    TO TOWN ALL GREEN
WITH SEEDLING RICE
              BAKUSUI

VANISHING SPRINGTIME . . .
   WISTFULLY
    THE LONELY WIDOW
POUTS AT HER MIRROR
              SEIBI

BLOWN CHERRY-BLOSSOMS
   FALL AND FLOAT
    UPON THE COLD
RICE-PADDY WATERS
              KYOROKU

THE GAY WATERWHEEL
   IN THE VALLEY
    POURS PETALS
FROM MOUNTAIN CHERRIES
              CHOGETSU

Summer

O SPRINGTIME TWILIGHT . . .
   PRECIOUS MOMENT
   WORTH TO ME
A THOUSAND PIECES

SOTOBA

REPLY:

O SUMMER TWILIGHT . . .
   BUG-DEPRECIATED
   TO A
MERE FIVE HUNDRED

KIKAKU

BOUNCING BAMBOO DIPPER
   IN THE WATER-TUB . . .
   FOLLOWING
A FLY-AWAY BIRD

HORO

A BABY SPARROW . . .
  HOPPING
  WITH CURIOSITY
TO WATCH MY BRUSHWORK
                    SHOHA

HOW COOL...SWEET GRASSES
  SCYTHED IN FIELDS
  AT EARLY DAWN
ENTERING OUR GATE
                    BONCHO

ON THE GIDDY SWING . . .
  TINY GIRL-CHILD
  CLUTCHING TIGHT
HER SPRAY OF BLOSSOMS
                    ISSA

AH ROADSIDE SCARECROW
  WE'VE HARDLY
  STARTED GABBING . . .
AND I HAVE TO GO
                    IZEN

19

PERHAPS THIS VOICELESS
   WANDERER DREAMS
   OF FLOWERS . . .
BUTTERFLY DOZER
               REIKAN

SOMETIMES THE FARMER
   TROTS OUT TO SEE
   HIS SCARECROW . . .
SLOWLY HE WALKS BACK
               BUSON

THAT DARK WATERFOWL
   ALTHOUGH APPEARING
   WEIGHTED . . .
SEE HOW IT CAN FLOAT!
               ONITSURA

AH BOLD NIGHTINGALE . . .
   EVEN BEFORE
   HIS LORDSHIP
YOU WON'T MEND YOUR SONG
               ISSA

THAT FAT OLD BULL-FROG
   SAT THERE STARING
   BACK AT ME
WITH A SOUR FACE
              ISSA

IN FLAT SUNSET LIGHT
   A BUTTERFLY
   WANDERING
DOWN THE CITY STREET
             KIKAKU

SOMEONE IS WALKING
   OVER THE WOODEN
   BRIDGE . . . HEAR
THE DEEP FROG-SILENCE
             RYOTO

A WAGON RUMBLING . . .
   AND OUT FROM
   SILENT GRASSES
A SUDDEN BUTTERFLY
             SHOHA

INTO THE BLINDING
   SETTING SUN THE
   SCARECROW STARES . . .
STILL INDIFFERENT
SHIRAO

GAY . . . AFFECTIONATE . . .
   WHEN I'M REBORN
   I PRAY TO BE A
WHITE-WING BUTTERFLY
ISSA

SQUATTING LIKE BUDDHA:
   BUT BITTEN
   BY MOSQUITOES
IN MY NIRVANA
OEMARU

AT THE ANCIENT SHRINE
   TARNISHED GOLD-FOIL . . .
   AND GREEN LEAVES
AWAKENING TIME
CHORA

EVEN WITH INSECTS . . .
   SOME ARE HATCHED
   OUT MUSICAL . . .
SOME, ALAS, TONE-DEAF
         ISSA

PLANTED ROWS OF BEANS
   AND RANDOM CLUMPS
   OF LILIES . . .
PROSPEROUS ISLET!
         SHIKI

NIGHTINGALE WEEPING
   AND CEASELESS OCEAN
   MOANING . . .
SOON O SOON THE DAWN
         SHIRAO

IN SUMMER MOONLIGHT . . .
   GLITTERING BROOKLET
   RUNNING
DOWN OUR VILLAGE STREET
         SHIRAO

TWO JADE-GREEN HILLTOPS
   STAND IN THEIR
   SUMMER LEAFAGE
MIRROR-IMAGES
         KYORAI

YELLOW FIREFLY . . .
   LITTLE LAMP-FLAME
   THAT TO THE
HUMAN TOUCH IS CHILL
         SHIKI

SUNNY FIELDS AND WARM . . .
   SEE THE MONK'S FACE
   PEEPING OUT
FROM THE TEMPLE FENCE
         ISSA

A CRABLET CRAWLING
   UP MY ANKLE-BONE . . .
   AH COOL
MEANDERING BROOK
         BASHO

24

IN MY NATIVE PLACE
   THERE'S THIS PLANT:
   AS PLAIN AS GRASS
BUT BLOOMS LIKE HEAVEN
               ISSA

PITIFUL BLIND CHILD . . .
   AND SO BRIEF
   THE ROSE OF SHARON
GARLANDING HER PORCH
               SHIRAO

DAYLIGHT AT THE INN . . .
   THROUGH MY LOOPED
   MOSQUITO NETS
A MORNING-GLORY
               SHIRO

TWILIGHT WATERING . . .
   AND PLEASE,
   A COOLING SPRINKLE
FOR WRENS AND CRICKETS
               KIKAKU

25

HAVING TUMBLED OFF
  HIS GRASS-BLADE . . .
  THE FIREFLY
BUZZES UP AGAIN

BASHO

MOONLIGHT NIGHTINGALE
  CASTS A WHISTLING
  LINE OF SOUND
OVER THE MILLPOND

BASHO

AS LIGHTNING FLASHES . . .
  ZIG-ZAG SCREECHES
  OF THE HERON
FLYING IN THE DARK

BASHO

HEREBY I ASSIGN,
  IN PERPETUITY,
  TO WIT :
TO THIS BIRD THIS FENCE

ISSA

STUBBORN WOODPECKER . . .
  STILL HAMMERING
  AT TWILIGHT
AT THAT SINGLE SPOT
                        ISSA

AT SILENT NOONTIDE . . .
  FAR ACROSS
  THE FLOWER-FIELDS
HEAR THE SIGHING SEA
                        BUSON

HEAR THE HUMMING
  AS HONEYSUCKLE
  PETALS FALL . . .
DISTURBED MOSQUITOS
                        BUSON

THE SICKLY ORCHID
  THAT I TENDED SO . . .
  AT LAST
THANKS ME WITH A BUD
                        TAIGI

POT-IMPRISONED NOW . . .
PALELY DREAMING
OCTOPUS
IN SUMMER MOONLIGHT
BASHO

CURLED ON THE FAN . . .
AHA! I'VE CAUGHT YOU
TOM-CAT
FAST ASLEEP AGAIN!
ISSA

HIGH SUN STILL BURNING
IN THE FALCON'S
EYES . . . DOWN TO
MY EARTH-BOUND WRIST
TAIRA

BUT SEE THE MOUNTAIN . . .
SHAKING WITH THE
WAVES OF HEAT
WHERE DAY HAS GONE
ONITSURA

28

FLOATING BUTTERFLY
   WHEN YOU DANCE
   BEFORE MY EYES . . .
ISSA, MAN OF MUD

        ISSA

SUPERNATURAL
   COOL BREEZE . . .
   BUDDHA'S PARADISE
MUST LIE THATAWAY

        ISSA

INSECTS POOR INSECTS . . .
   HOW WISE TO PURGE
   YOUR KARMA
CRYING PENITENCE

        OTOKUNI

WE HARK TO CRICKET
   AND TO HUMAN
   CHIRPINGS . . . WITH
EARS SO DIFFERENT

        WAFU

SLOW HOT SILENT HOURS . . .
   IN THE AFTERNOON
   A PHEASANT
SETTLES ON THE BRIDGE
               BUSON

THE SOFT SUMMER MOON . . .
   WHO IS IT MOVES
   IN WHITE THERE . . .
ON THE OTHER BANK?
               CHORA

AT MY HUT I FEAR
   ALL I CAN REALLY
   TEMPT YOU WITH . . .
SMALLISH MOSQUITOES
               BASHO

WHILE I SWOOP MY NET,
   DELIBERATE
   BUTTERFLY . . .
YOU NEVER HURRY
               GARAKU

AH . . . MORNING-GLORY
GLOWING WITH
THE INDIGO
OF SOME MOUNTAIN
                    BUSON

SILENT THE GARDEN
WHERE THE
CAMELLIA-TREE
OPENS ITS WHITENESS
                    ONITSURA

FROM THE DAY IT'S BORN
OF ABANDONED
STICKS AND RAGS . . .
ELDERLY SCARECROW
                    NYOFU

NOW THIS GOOD SEA-SLUG
HAS BOTH HEAD
AND TAIL . . . BUT GOD
KNOWS WHICH IS WHICH
                    KYORAI

35

THAT NIGHT WHEN I HAD
    SOLD MY LOWER
    FIELD . . . I LAY
WAKEFUL FROM FROG-CALLS
              HOKUSHI

HEY! WHY DON'T YOU HELP
    THAT BUZZING
    HORSE-FLY OPEN
THE STICKING SKYLIGHT?
              ISSA

DAWN-TWITTERING BIRDS . . .
    OUR OVERNIGHT
    BIG-CITY GUEST
ALONE IS STIRRING
              SHOHA

TENDER BAMBOO-SHOOTS
    AND BABY'S TENDER
    GUM-PINKS . . .
TINY TOOTH-CUTTING
              RANSETSU

BOUNCING THE BALL . . .
SHE BENDS TO MAKE
A FACE AT HER
MEOWING KITTEN

ISSA

IN THE SUDDEN BURST
OF SUMMER RAIN . . .
WIND-BLOWN BIRDS
CLUTCHING AT GRASSES

BUSON

LIKE A BUTTERFLY . . .
THE PILGRIM'S
TOMBOY YOUNGSTER
TROTS UNEVENLY

SHIKI

THE MONKS EXHIBIT
BUDDHA'S IMAGE . . .
SPARROWS TOO
ARE DAWN-LIGHT LOOKERS

ISSA

Autumn

ON THE EBB-TIDE BEACH
   THE HURRYING CRAB
   STOPS SHORT . . .
THERE IS A FOOTPRINT!
             ROFU

BRACED IN THE WATERS . . .
   SCARECROW IN
   THE FLOODED FIELD
GRIMLY ENDURES IT
             SHIKI

AH MY FOREST HUT . . .
   WHERE THE FRIENDLY
   WOODPECKER
KNOCKS AT DOOR AND POST
             BASHO

ON THIS STILL WATER
   SEE WHERE
   HIS REFLECTION
MEETS THE WATERFOWL
               MAHARA

QUITE THE STUPIDEST
   OF ALL LIVING
   CREATURES IS
A DRY OLD SCARECROW
               SHIKI

AUTUMN NIGHTS ARE COLD...
   CRUSHING THE TINY
   CHILD TO ME ...
WARM LOVELY YOUNGLING
               SHIKI

BEHIND THE TWISTED
   BRANCHES WITH
   THE EAGLE'S NEST ...
RED SINKING SUN-BALL
               BONCHO

AS I LIGHT THE LAMP
   BEHOLD . . . TO EVERY
   SINGLE DOLL
ITS OWN REAL SHADOW
SHIKI

MOTHER LOST, LONG GONE . . .
   AT THE DEEP DARK SEA
   I STARE . . .
AT THE DEEP DARK SEA
ISSA

AH SACRED SWALLOW . . .
   TWITTERING OUT
   FROM YOUR NEST IN
GREAT BUDDHA'S NOSTRIL
ISSA

TEA-KETTLE HANDLE . . .
   I'LL CUT IT FROM
   THE BAMBOO
OF THAT BUBBLING WREN
KIKAKU

WEEPING . . . WILLOWS
KNEEL HERE BY
THE WATERSIDE
MINGLING LONG GREEN HAIR
KYORAI

GATHERING STARLINGS
CRY AS THEY
SPRINKLE BERRIES
FROM THE AUTUMN TREE
SHIKI

SILVERY HERRINGS
POURING . . .
A LIVE WATERFALL
FROM NET TO BASKET
KIKAKU

AH LEAFLESS WILLOW . . .
BENDING OVER
THE DRY POOL
OF STRANDED BOULDERS
BUSON

41

O YOU SNUB-NOSE DOLL!
   MAYBE YOUR
   MOTHER DIDN'T
PINCH AND PULL ENOUGH
              BUSON

PERCHED ON THE BAMBOO
   MARKER OF A
   NEW-DUG GRAVE . . .
THE WAITING DRAGONFLY
              KITO

ALL ALONG THE BEACH . . .
   PLOVERS PLAYING
   AT SOME GAME
INVOLVING WET-FOOT
              BUSON

WITH PHILOSOPHY
   HE CONTEMPLATES
   THE MOUNTAIN . . .
OLD PROFESSOR FROG

              ISSA

AT THE SETTING SUN . . .
WASHING DOWN
HIS WEARY HORSE
IN THE AUTUMN SEA

SHIKI

ON THIS PLAIN OF MIST
NOTHING BUT FLAT
ENDLESSNESS . . .
AND RED-RISING SUN

SHIRO

RISING HARVEST MOON . . .
FROM THIS HUT
AS YET UNWALLED
I WILL VIEW IT WELL

SHIRAO

BITTER BROKEN REEDS . . .
DAY IN DAY OUT
THE FALLEN
FLOAT AWAY . . . AFAR

RANKO

PENETRATING HOT
   SEPTEMBER SUN . . .
  ON MY SKIN
FEEL THE COOLING BREEZE
           BASHO

I AM GROWING OLD . . .
   O SWEET BIRD
   DISAPPEARING
INTO AUTUMN DUSK
           BASHO

WHO IS THAT, HUDDLED
   IN A STRAW-COAT . . .
   STARING AT OUR
HOLIDAY PARADE?
           BASHO

SEE THIS DRAGONFLY . . .
   HIS FACE IS
   PRACTICALLY
NOTHING ELSE BUT EYES
           CHISOKU

COMPANION CUCKOO . . .
   KEEP YOUR EYE COCKED
   ON MY HUT
UNTIL I COME BACK

              ISSA

REDDISH MORNING SKY . . .
   RAIN FOR YOU TODAY
   I GUESS,
LITTLE LUCKY SNAIL!

              ISSA

WITHIN PALE SILENCE
   SPREADING FROM
   EVENING MOONLIGHT . . .
SUDDEN CICADA

             HAJIN

WET MORNING GARDEN . . .
   MY SUNNY
   CHRYSANTHEMUMS
ARE SEA-MIST-SHROUDED

             SAMPU

WITH THE MOON-RISING . . .
   LEAF AFTER LEAF
   AFTER LEAF
FALLS FLUTTERING DOWN
          SHIKI

I DIDN'T ENTER . . .
   BUT I STOPPED
   IN REVERENCE . . .
AUTUMN-LEAF TEMPLE
          BUSON

SUDDEN RADIANCE . . .
   AFTER OCTOBER
   RAINSTORM
RE-REDDENED PEPPERS
          BUSON

THE PEOPLE, WE KNOW . . .
   BUT THESE DAYS
   EVEN SCARECROWS
DO NOT STAND UPRIGHT
          ISSA

ONLY WITHERED GRASSES
   IN YOUR CAGE? . . .
  O CRICKET CAPTIVE
MY APOLOGIES!

               SHOHA

FROM FISH-BOAT TORCHES
   SPARKS ARE FALLING . . .
  POOR TETHERED
SCORCH-FACE CORMORANTS

               KAKEI

THIS IS MY OWN PLACE . . .
   MUD-HUT AND
  COMPANION TREE
SHEDDING AUTUMN LEAVES

               CHORA

FROM THE HAUNTED HUT
   SMOKE IS SEEPING
  IN THE RAIN . . .
SOMEONE IS INSIDE!

               BUSON

SEPTEMBER LIGHTNING . . .
   WHITE CALLIGRAPHY
     ON HIGH
SILHOUETTES THE HILL
          JOSO

SEE . . . SIX GAPING BEAKS
   WAITING FOR
    THE MOTHER-BIRD
IN COLD AUTUMN RAIN
          ISSA

SILENT AUTUMN AIR . . .
   HERE AND THERE
    AMONG THE HILLS
RISING THIN BLUE SMOKES
          GYODAI

THE FISHERMAN'S HUT . . .
   WHERE LIVELY CRICKETS
    MINGLE NOW
WITH DRYING SHRIMP
          BASHO

ANNIVERSARY OF DEATH

RISING AUTUMN MOON . . .
   LIGHTING IN MY
   LAP THIS YEAR
NO PALE SICKLY CHILD
          ONITSURA

FOR FALL FESTIVALS
   OUR RELIGIOUS
   DRAGONFLIES
DON RED GARMENTS TOO
          ISSA

WILD GEESE O WILD GEESE
   WERE YOU LITTLE
   FELLOWS TOO . . . WHEN
YOU FLEW FROM HOME?
          ISSA

BY ABANDONED ROADS
   THIS LONELY
   POET MARCHES
INTO AUTUMN DUSK
          BASHO

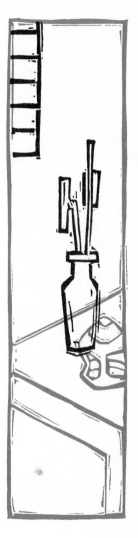

Winter

TELL ME: WHERE DOES THIS
    UNEXPECTED COLD SNAP
    COME FROM . . .
WEATHERWISE SCARECROW?
                  ISSA

WINE-DRINKING-WAKEFUL
    ALL ALONE THAT
    BITTER NIGHT
I STARTED AT SNOWFALL
                BASHO

SNOW-ISOLATED . . .
    ONCE MORE I PRESS
    MY BACK AGAINST
MY THINKING-POST
                BASHO

BACK TO MY HOME TOWN
AND BURIAL
IN MY HUT . . .
FIVE COLD FEET OF SNOW
ISSA

WINTER WOODCUTTER . . .
WHEN YOUR AXE CUTS
HOME I SCENT
UNEXPECTED SPRING
BUSON

MY OLD FATHER TOO
LOOKED LONG ON THESE
WHITE MOUNTAINS
THROUGH LONELY WINTERS
ISSA

FEEBLE FEEBLE SUN . . .
IT CAN SCARCELY
STRETCH ACROSS
WINTER-WASTED FIELDS
BAKUSUI

WINTER-SOLITARY . . .
　I FIND SOLACE
　IN THIS OLD
CHINESE-PAINTED PINE
　　　　　BASHO

THE MOURNING FATHER
DEEP UNDER ASHES . . .
　BURNING CHARCOAL
　CHILLED NOW BY
HIS HISSING TEARS
　　　　　BASHO

IN THE RAINY DAWN
　SEE WHERE I CREPT
　OUT OF BED . . .
HOLE IN THE BEDCLOTHES
　　　　　JOSO

A MOUNTAIN HAMLET . . .
　UNDER THE GREAT
　WHITE SNOWDRIFT
A GURGLING BROOK
　　　　　SHIKI

52

AT FREEZING MIDNIGHT
  HEAR THAT RAT
  GO RUMMAGING . . .
DIRTY KITCHEN DISHES
                    BUSON

EVEN MY LAMP-LIGHT . . .
  HIBERNATING
  IN A FROZEN
WINTER-WHITE HALO
                    YAHA

LAST NIGHT A SNOWFALL . . .
  TODAY CLEAR COBALT
  HEAVEN AND
WHITE-MANTLED PINES
                    ROKA

A BITTER NIGHT . . . BUT
  LONG PRACTICE
  WITH COLD HUNGER
PERMITTED ME TO SLEEP
                    IZEN

53

SOFT SNOWFLAKES SETTLE
  DOWN ON THESE
  UNSTIRRING DUCKS . . .
A WORLD OF SILENCE
                    SHIKI

WET SNOW IS SWEEPING
  OVER THE RED-BERRY
  BUSH . . .
TWO SPARROWS CHIRPING
                    SHIKI

OVER AND OVER
  FROM MY BED
  I ASK MY NURSE:
NOW, HOW DEEP THE SNOW?
                    SHIKI

AT THIS DREARY INN
  A HOUND KEEPS
  WAILING . . . LIKE ME
LONELY IN THE RAIN?
                    BASHO

THE VERY PLANETS
    GLEAMING THROUGH
    ITS SILHOUETTE . . .
FROZEN WILLOW-TREE
                    CHORA

EVERY SINGLE STAR
    IS QUIVERING NOW
    WITH LIGHT . . .
O HOW BITTER COLD
                    TAIGI

BRIGHT SOUL OF WINTER . . .
    MOONLIGHT
    PUNCTUATED BY
PATTERING HAILSTONES
                    GYODAI

BITTER WINTER WIND . . .
    WON'T IT BLOW
    RIGHT OFF THE SKY
THAT DAY-OLD CRESCENT?
                    KAKEI

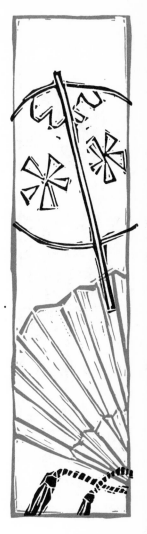

NOW AT DAWN THE TIDE
   FLOATS INCOMING
   LAYERS ON
OUR NIGHT-FROZEN COVE
            SHIKI

POLISHING THE BUDDHA . . .
   AND WHY NOT
   MY PIPE AS WELL
FOR THE HOLIDAY?
            ISSA

ON A RAINY DAY
   THE DRIPPING
   SCARECROWS SEEM LIKE
ORDINARY MEN
            SEIBI

REMEMBERING
   THEIR PAINTED FACES . . .
   SHE UNWRAPPED
HER OLD PAIR OF DOLLS
            BUSON

IT IS WARM TODAY . . .
   BUT I THINK
   I FEEL THE CHILL
OF THAT WINTER SUN
              ONITSURA

CHILDREN, COME ON OUT :
   CLATTERING
   ALONG THE LANE
SEE . . . IT'S HAILING PEARLS
           BASHO

ICY WINTER NIGHT . . .
   I UNFREEZE
   THE WRITING-BRUSH
WITH MY TWO GOOD TEETH
           BUSON

OUT OVER THE LAKE
   LONG COLD
   HOLLOW EMPTINESS . . .
A SOLITARY CROW
           SHIKI

THOSE TWO TIRED DOLLS
   IN THE CORNER
   THERE . . . AH YES
THEY ARE MAN AND WIFE
                    ISSA

SILLY HAILSTONES . . .
   FLEEING INTO
   MY FIREPLACE
FAST AS THEY CAN RUN
                    ISSA

IN ICY MOONLIGHT
   PIN-POINT-PATTERING
   PEBBLES
CRUNCHING UNDERFOOT
                   BUSON

COLD WINTER RAIN-LINES
   ARE LIFTED
   HORIZONTAL
BY THE HOWLING GALE
                 KYORAI

WITH THIS HAT BLOWN OFF
   THE STIFF-NECKED
    SCARECROW STANDS HERE
QUITE DISCOMFITED
                   BUSON

ICY-WINTER NIGHT . . .
   PERHAPS THE WATER-
    BIRDS, LIKE ME,
ARE LAKESIDE HUDDLERS
                  ROTSU

DARKENING SNOW-CLOUDS . . .
   OVER THIS WAITING
    LAKE AND LAND
BLACK BIRDS WHIMPERING
               OTOKUNI

BLUE-SHADOW-BOLTED . . .
   THE CASTLE GATE
    OF EDO
IN FROZEN MOONLIGHT
              KIKAKU

MY NEIGHBORS HATE ME . . .
   HEAR THEM BANG
   AND RATTLE PANS
IN THE ICY NIGHT

BUSON

THAT SNOTTY URCHIN
   LEFT UNPICKED
   BY EITHER TEAM . . .
AH THE BITTER COLD!

SHIKI

BEFORE THE BUDDHA
   EVEN GOOD SPARROWS
   BOW . . . PARENTS
AND CHILDREN BOTH

ISSA

A HARSH-RASPING SAW
   MUSIC OF
   COLD POVERTY
IN WINTER MIDNIGHT

BUSON

YEAR-END REVELLING . . .
STILL IN PILGRIM'S
CAPE MUST I
ROAM MY ENDLESS ROAD
BASHO

SINCE DEAR BASHO DIED
WHAT POEM-MAKER
DARES TO WRITE
"YEAR-END REVELLING"?
BUSON

DEATH-SONG

I WAS ALLOTTED
TWO AUTUMNS MORE
THAN AVERAGE MAN
THE HARVEST MOON
SAIKAKU

DEATH-SONG

ON THE LAST LONG ROAD
WHEN I FALL AND
FAIL TO RISE . . .
I'LL BED WITH FLOWERS
SORA